The Cat Outside His Door

Poems After Roethke

The Cat Outside His Door

Poems After Roethke

New and Selected Poems

Fred Wolven

LAKE & EMERALD PUBLICATIONS

Copyright © 2014 Fred Wolven
All rights reserved.

No part of this publication may be reproduced, in any form or by any means, without the prior permission in writing, except for brief passages in a published review.

> Published by Lake and Emerald Publications, LLC
> www.lepublications.com
> in association with Ann Arbor Review Press

Library of Congress Control Number: 2014947994

Paperback ISBN: 978-0-9906768-5-0
  ebook ISBN: 978-0-9906768-0-5

Cover Photo: Karyn M. Bruce
Used with permission.

Poems in this book previously appeared in The Adirondack Review; Ann Arbor Review: an International Journal; Asili: The Journal of Multicultural Heartspeak; The Clockwise Cat: A Progressive Literary Magazine; Ken*again, the literary magazine; Mountain Valley Review; Poetry Life & Times. Selected poems have also appeared in After the Death of Theodore Roethke (Tampa), Another Roethke Round: Memories and Motion (Mountain Valley Review), and In Glass Fields (Lake & Emerald Publications)

Contents

Foreword ix

Preface xi

A Movement After Roethke

A Movement After Roethke 17

A Small Gift For Jason 18

Cutting Shrubs 20

After The Death Of Theodore Roethke 21

Roethke, Revisited 23

Each Root, Each Stem, Each Leaf… 25

A Poem After Roethke's *Rose* 26

The Cat Outside His Door

The Cat Outside His Door, # 1 31

The Cat Outside His Door, # 2 32

The Cat Outside His Door, # 3 33

The Cat Outside His Door, # 4 34

The Cat Outside His Door, # 5 35

The Cat Outside His Door, # 6 36

The Cat Outside His Door, # 7 37

The Cat Outside His Door, # 8 38

There Was a Cat Outside His Door

There Was a Cat Outside His Door, # 1 41

There Was a Cat Outside His Door, # 2 42

There Was a Cat Outside His Door, # 3 43

There Was a Cat Outside His Door, # 4 44

There Was a Cat Outside His Door, # 5 45

There Was a Cat Outside His Door, # 6 46
There Was a Cat Outside His Door, # 7 47
There Was a Cat Outside His Door, # 8 48
There Was a Cat Outside His Door, # 9 49
There Was a Cat Outside His Door, # 10 50
There Was a Cat Outside His Door, # 11 51
There Was a Cat Outside His Door, # 12 52
There Was a Cat Outside His Door, # 13 53

There's No Cat Outside My Door

There's No Cat Outside My Door, #1 57
There's No Cat Outside My Door, #2 58
There's No Cat Outside My Door, #3 59
There's No Cat Outside My Door, #4 60
There's No Cat Outside My Door, #5 61
There's No Cat Outside My Door, #6 62
There's No Cat Outside My Door, #7 63
There's No Cat Outside My Door, #8 64
There's No Cat Outside My Door, #9 65
There's No Cat Outside My Door, #10 66
There's No Cat Outside My Door, #11 67
There's No Cat Outside My Door, #12 68
There's No Cat Outside My Door, #13 69

Did You See That Cat?

Did You See That Cat? #1 73
Did You See That Cat? #2 74
Did You See That Cat? #3 75
Did You See That Cat? #4 76

Did You See That Cat? #5 77
Did You See That Cat? #6 78

Sitting With Theodore Roethke

Sitting With Theodore Roethke, #1 81
Sitting With Theodore Roethke, #2 82
Sitting With Theodore Roethke, #3 83

Theodore Roethke in Michigan

Theodore Roethke in Michigan, #1 87
Theodore Roethke in Michigan, #2 88
Theodore Roethke in Michigan, #3 89
Theodore Roethke in Michigan, #4 90

Sometimes Theodore Roethke Just Slips into a Poem Meant for Another

Sometimes Theodore Roethke Just Slips into a Poem Meant for Another 93
It Sounds Like Your Woodpecker Has Moved Into My Tree 94
The Hillside Was Covered 95
Cats And Mothers Grow Somewhat Alike 97
Sometimes, During The Rain 98
Three Days Before Theodore Roethke Died 100
Epilogue: Somewhere, Somehow, Theodore, I Know 103
About The Author 106

Foreword

By Duane Locke *

Language poetry, an end-of-the-century fashion, with its supposed innovations which really were a clearing away of poetic debris such as moribund expressive means, restrictions that were prevalent but never valid, feelings that had become standardized formulas rather than personal, unique, singular involved emotions in favor of apparently new post Ferdinand De Saussure linguistic modes modified by post-structuralism, philosophically underpinned by deconstructionism, and in their following the vague and general expression of Ezra Pound "To make it new" introduced new poetic gadgets. Among these gadgets such as "The New Sentence," turning words upside down, attaching marginalia with a scattering of disconnected letters, sous rapture, and what was called "writing through."

In "writing through," the poet would take a text of Ludwig Wittgenstein along with Gertrude Stein, would annotate, delete, add, change and through a stress on the materiality of the signifier come through with a new text. Fred Wolven is expressing his homage to a preceding poet, Theodore Roethke, in a different manner and with a different relationship than the "writing through" au courant gadgeteenism.

In our age when poetry in many hinterland locations as well as the mega-metropolis has become a burlesque show performance, replete with a surfeit of clown antics and noisy acrobatics, Fred writes with a soft tone, a tone slightly above a whisper that ingratiates with its soothing, yet exciting, invisibility, and we are transported on an immobile journey that is a new kind of motion and it is a journey to everywhere although we remain in a strange stasis. We are cast into a disclosement, the revelation of a muted and unmated poetic excitement.

Our conceptual categories that posit binary oppositions vanish in the processes of the poems, the subjects and objects disappear into new substantial appearances.

A central occurrent in the poems is a cat. A cat that is not a cat, a cat that is a cat, a cat that ultimately is a hyper, super, or symbolic cat, even an anagogic cat. The cat becomes a Greek chorus, but a special type of Greek chorus, a chorus of sounds and simultaneously of silence. A cat's presence or the cat's absence is a running commentary, often a commentary of silence, a silence that speaks more than sounds.

The poems are the narrator's involvement with the poetry and life and earth of Theodore Roethke. Roethke has become an aura, an emanation. Roethke, among vegetation, has overcome the slave mentality's abolition of the plant when observing the plant, has overcome the biologist's substituting information to replace the life of the plant, has become personally and intensely involved with and exalted by the individual existence of the plant. In Roethke, a plant is not a plant, a plant is a plant, a plant is a hyper plant, and the narrators partake of apotheosis and authentic mystic existence of the plant.

The ardent and attentive perception of Roethke attuned to the minutiae, its glory and grandness, of nature is transferred to the narrator who because Roethke lived has become more alive in his life. A largeness is found in the small, a largeness that surpasses in its granting of love what the unloved largeness cannot do. It is Roethke privileging the here over the not here, and this privileging has enhanced and expanded quotidian existence, and transformed the narrator.

So, we the reader can participate in how an authentic and intensive life, without being aware of what is taking place, can transform another life, and how we can be transformed by the transformation.

*Duane Locke, former Poet in Residence, now Professor Emeritus, University of Tampa, editor and publisher of Poetry Review and UT Review, is an award winning poet, prize-winning photographer and noted contemporary folk artist.

Preface

I trust that your reading of this collection will extend your interest in or introduce you to the fascinating poetic world of Theodore Roethke while *bringing you more directly into the puzzling, beautiful, natural, and amazing world of my and his use of nature's creatures, a searching for the sometimes allusive answer to the essence of the "I" in* **myself***, and into the continuing search for and recognition of love and like which is all around us.* Such is the content of my poetic endeavors; such is the content of my world – the world of the Midwest, the world of Roethke, the world of his Northwest scene, and of mine here in the Southeast both near the oceans. *These are the worlds in which many of us live – those filled with nature's abundance and glow and which are also peopled by many disconcerting questions about existence and love, et al.*

Born in Michigan, Roethke's native state and a student of a then small state university, I first discovered his writings through readings in British and American literary and news periodicals. Immediately caught by the quality of his use of nature, by his continuing struggle to grasp a more complete understanding of himself, and by the commonalities in place and location use and their influence in his writing, I started a life-long study of his work. Aided initially by a friend's knowledge of Saginaw, Michigan, Roethke's birthplace, and of his poetry, by my spending a few years living in that city not far from where Roethke grew up, near the fields wherein Roethke roamed as a youngster, down the street from the Roethke family florist shop, and in the area of the cemetery where the poet rests today, I took in, first hand, his deep Michigan roots and his foundational interest in nature, and I realized the impact Roethke was having and would continue to have on contemporary poetry and on me.

Upon commencing an extended teaching career, I began using several Roethke poems and ideas (on poetics and learning) to instruct, to enlighten, and to help develop poetic appreciation and literary understanding in my many, many students. Naturally, also, my own writing started revealing the influence of Roethke, especially since I also wrote extensively using nature's best – the tiny creatures, the varied birds, the many trees, roots and leaves, the streams and water, and the varied fish and other wildlife also filling my childhood and early adult years in Michigan – as image, symbol and for portraits in my work. Roethke had become my not so silent mentor.

One of my professors was kind in his assessment of my first critical paper focused on Roethke – a brief analysis of the poems Roethke published in periodicals in 1963, the year of his untimely death from a heart attack. From that year on I read critics commenting on Roethke's work, and often I find they just plain lack sufficient insight to be able to assess the exacting and powerful influence he has had on contemporary poets and poetry. All too often they were either too vain, too self-centered, or just plain lacking in sufficient understanding to acknowledge the fact that Roethke was in the process of becoming more substantial than most of them. Or they just could not get pass the fact of earlier poets' influence in Roethke's works, or they considered him not much more than a 'garden variety' verse writer. Whatever the reason, they were often incorrect in their assessments and very incomplete in their observations.

At any rate, in the early 1960s Duane Locke created a stirring little magazine, *Poetry Review*, at the University of Tampa (Florida) wherein he published many then developing poets – Amiri Baraka, Peter Wild, Diane Wakoski, Coleman Barks, David Ignatow, and Sam Cornish, among others, and his own aspiring student writers. He also published the first of my early then 'annual' Roethke influenced poems. Aided and abetted by some success in my publishing in magazines; by my own students' successes in their writing development; in my successfully helping create, edit and publish a literary review in Ann Arbor in 1967 and my ever expanding poetic curiosity and fascination with Roethke's own poems and his creative ideas, I have continued my interest in Roethke's work. And several decades later, this interest and influence remains.

Shortly before the time of his death in the summer of 1963, students of a west coast university produced a wonderful black and white film (*In a Dark Time*) of Roethke reading and performing his poetry in the Puget Sound area of Washington. (While his death ended his very successful teaching career at the University of Washington, it didn't his influence.) In the film there is a glimpse of a cat visible through the screen door outside the living room in which Roethke is being filmed. Somehow, that cat caught my attention, and so, over the years, Roethke and that cat and other cats have become inspirations for, objects in, and resources for some of my poems – thus the various series in this collection which reference both the poet and the cat. Perhaps there are yet more poems to be written treating some aspect of these subjects, as well as other of nature's elements, perhaps not; I can't be sure.

Now retired from academic life, the teaching portion, and having helped re-establish the sixties started journal as an international poetry journal (and ezine), I continue the quest for fashioning the just right poem, and gaining a better understanding of the enigma that is mine and that which was Roethke's own. After all, he once said, *"What I love is near at hand."* Thus, there is so much yet left to be explored; plus, as he noted, *"Being, not doing, is my first joy."* What with nature's beauty all around, and my continuing to reach out and touch, feel and appreciate such, along with having opted to re-open myself to love and life, and still seeking to more fully define my identity, I *write on, write on....*

As a result, in my allusions to Roethke, his life and work, the connections therein made fashion a creative tension between us in subject matter, language and ideas. I therefore extend to you an invitation to explore these with me, for until one has sampled the new bottled wine batch, one is unable to compliment the quality of the vintage.

And...

A Note of Thanks

There are many people to acknowledge for special support in the creation of this collection: first, a friend from Saginaw, Michigan, who introduced me to much about Roethke and the area in which he grew up and which played such an influential part in his life and writings. Then, too, a couple editors who were the first to publish many of my earlier "Roethke" influenced poems written in a much more open form and format and to *Duane Locke* for introducing this collection. And two other women in my life: *Karyn* and *Chris* for reading and providing feedback on this mss. and suffering through my years of teaching Roethke's works. Also, my three daughters all of whom were kind in listening to my reading and talking of Roethke over the years. And now, even my granddaughter starting to learn of Roethke and my poems. And *Carmen*, without whom I might never have completed this collection. And various other editors, publishers and friends for their insight and acknowledgement over the years. Finally, to *Richard*, who stepped in to act as my publishing editor when all others seemed to disappear. Thanks.

A Movement After Roethke

A Movement After Roethke

i followed you to the cemetery;
they, who brought you here, didn't know,
& now, though I have some regret
in having missed you
when walking these same streets,
& my daughters still buy flowers from **Roethke's**,
having first read your poems in an English newspaper
while standing in a cigar shop in your town,
i am able to pass by the cemetery
where they left you
near where i used to live,
& i remember, without even turning to look,
you spoke only of the joy, the pleasure
in a sudden discovery of the pike
nearly motionless in the stream
hidden under an overhanging bank,
in the gentle touching of ferns
dropping from the basket suspended
over the uncurtained window,
in the one sensuous moment of physical love,
in the sound of a bird's song growing in early summer
in the east-spreading light,
& that is nearly enough.

A Small Gift For Jason

for Jason, my nephew

1.
outside snow crystals
cover the brown grass,
& ice-glazed sidewalks
surround the stone library walls
as i work in Roethke's home town
reading essays nearly forgotten
in the years since his death.

2.
setting the prose aside,
i search back room shelves,
find his collected poems,
pour over now familiar lines
& remember the still fresh images
of flowers, roots & love,
sensing again the feelings,
the strong pulse of a man
at once wild with the fever of life,
& yet, in those same stanzas,
barely able to discern a difference
between the ecstasy of physical pleasure
& the note of madness in extreme despair

3.
did he intend i should question
his perceptions, his exaggerations
so vividly offered in poem
after poem, line after line,
or rather, should i always know,
as perhaps only he did

moving, often confused, in a confusing world,
which sense was which, his or mine,
either in the despairing relief
found in real sensual acts
or in the joy possible & expressed
in a release of anger

so long held in, then presented
in these pieces, these fragments
remaining after many years

4.
following a morning of reading,
recollecting & writing, i relax
& leave the store-walled rooms
passing again through this
city of a poet's childhood,
place of my earlier days,
& walk toward the main street
looking for a small gift for Jason,
my nephew, having meandered
in the childhood library of Roethke
a master craftsman and my mentor

Cutting Shrubs

broken branches
lie fallen on the grass
leaves turning brown.
shallow roots
of small flowering shrubs
pull out easily
as i tug.

i work my way
around the house
trimming back dwarf trees,
old & new bushes
& large evergreens.

insects near
land on green leaves;
a cicada flits
from ground to branch
& back to dirt again.

i leave the front hedge
for last; it needs more
attention, the jutting
new growth
gone wild this month.

& while i cut & shape
i remember
how Roethke
had to redo
his cuttings later,
changing nature's course.

After The Death Of Theodore Roethke

i moved
walking near the site
of his father's greenhouse
trying
to enter his world
to sift thru
the florist's heap
thru the roses
the tulips & geraniums

passing
again & again
outside the gates
of Oakwood
unable to enter
unable
to approach his grave

why does
he move in
the mystic night
beyond me
within a circle
connecting our childhoods
into a slow early winter
with its shallow freeze
chilling wind
& meditative mood

when he passes
will i know
will petals
drop on his grave
untended

will i recognize
his twisting shape
his dancing spirit
will I only pass
once more around
outside the gate
alone
unfound

Roethke, Revisited

1.
i read about his childhood
after reading his poems
& then
only after he died

2.
they laid him to rest
a few miles from the florist shop
bearing his family name
though that has no significance now
still those same kinds of
roses, tulips, & geraniums,
or their growing & wilting,
were strong influences
part of the reason
he credited the 'muck & mire'
of Michigan as being very real
in his work
in his careful renderings of plants,
roots & flowers,
portraits painted throughout his years
not so much from memory
but in an out-pouring of feelings
emotions choking
until released in verse

3.
he died suddenly
& they brought him home
one last time
placing his ashes
in the Oakwood plot
not too far from the house
i live in

4.
now
there are his many poems
& the strong ones
move off the pages
reach me when i read
pull at me
steadily like a giant magnet
& i feel close to him
in some way associated
at least entering into his world
making it mine
& in reading
i live a little more
with the feel of each line
each image
walk a little bit further
on his streets
in my time.

Each Root, Each Stem, Each Leaf...

as long as the black hole
does not enlarge & too quickly
swallow elements of our part
of the universe,
nor in the next rain
i am not stranded in a concrete
canyon then swept off my car roof
along the gutter to a huge drain
& dropping, like that time
in the dark unsure of my footing
i stumbled into an abandoned farm well,
& lose what breath i take,
from the real world each day.

yes, as long as now i can,
in reaching touch each leaf
of the ivy, the fern, the jade,
& the philodendron, & feel,
as he, my poet, did,
in the veins of these plants
a growing out of each root,
out of each stem,
each bud, each leaf,
that awakens in my world
each day
as when talking i pause
& in leaning in listen & hear you, Roethke,
speaking even as from inside plants.

A Poem After Roethke's *Rose*

When crossing through
the open meadow-like field
in its being populated
with wild flowers
especially Queen Anne's Lace
their carrot like roots
strengthening their stand
in the early summer Midwestern winds,
and their mini hot air balloon shape
canopy opening like parachutes,
here and there the delicate
Indian Pipe, more difficult in spotting
its bent over pipes resembling
cranes in feeding times, and further along
the occasional Trillium,
its large bright white petals
often earlier being a harbinger of spring
in Michigan acres.

It's no wonder I can spend
the whole morning or afternoon
meandering slowly around
in such acreage as this
not far removed from Roethke's
childhood haunts nearby
his boyhood home. Oh,
to have been his sidekick
during those young growing years
how much more I might
have learned up close and personal
of nature's unending wonders
of such a magnificent nurturing cycle
spread wide as the eye might see.

And then too, when venturing
over next to the close by woodlot's
meadow entering brook
zigzagging across my path
here and yonder
giving a child such as Theodore
and I another whole universe
for exploration right under
our noses so to speak
how much more amazing
an opportunity might a youngster have
to undercover the merits of spring
and summer days amid such splendor
such awe-striking wildflowers
and their artist splashed colors
and also able to visit the tiny creatures and critters
in, on and alongside the stream's
slow moving waters—
the spider movement of water bugs,
the dart, sudden stop, wiggling
of minnows, tadpoles stirring in side ponds,
and above the multiple butterflies,
and the bees and wasps alighting
to suckle the sweet nectar of flowering plants.
And less I forget is my occasional discovery
of the wild, prairie rose with its rose pink
petals peopling some roadside ditches
and their banks come along now into my view.

How could one not be struck
by such beauty so strong as almost
over-powering in its presence near me.
Such is the like of this common awe-striking
spectacle confronting me in these my learning years.

The Cat Outside His Door

The Cat Outside His Door, # 1

The cat just sits there looking in.
Once I stood in the middle of
a treed opening, just looking into
a Tennessee forest glen. Then I

was outside turning in. Now, I sit
alone inside, ten feet from you,
looking out into gentle October rains.
This space between us, like that

of dawn till dusk, fills & empties,
empties & fills, hour after hour,
& the silence weighing on me,
day after day, pulls me

deeper & deeper into the darkness. Like
Roethke's geranium, tossed out by a maid,
that rose I last bought you has withered
& died, browned & drooped;

so, you bagged & tagged it,
& put it out for the trash.

The Cat Outside His Door, # 2

He just sits there looking in.
Today I look carefully through
journal pages, checking for notes
from Roethke's lively meditations.

Yet, I notice that my lines are fewer,
the words more sparse, & even
the images not as quickly recorded.
I cannot find the song God has wrought.

Thinking it was you, I stewed, caught
& fought, then cursed, bent & bowed.
Too late alive, too far at five,
I did not know your love I'd lost.

Now, I do not know how to touch you,
though I'm willing to learn. Whether
I plead or only yearn, it is quite clear
what I tossed may be forever lost.

Still, I grope, I mourn; I wish, I curse;
I walk, I run; I kick, & yes, I even claw.

The Cat Outside His Door, # 3

Even now he just sits waiting, looking in.
The wall is sturdy, no rocks will fall;
the ledge is small, the movement slow.
A glimpse, a sparkle, a tear or two....

It makes little difference when I'm with you.
There's the turning sound;
as I pass round & round,
it grows louder & louder

filling my head, shoving aside
careful thoughts & lasting longer.
The spinning is more frequent,
the twists, the shapes, all move too;

the feeble efforts, the pills I take
do not stop the on-coming wall of water.
My hair's too thin, my legs too small,
& though I give my all, how can

I dismantle this my wall? Unlike Roethke's,
this dance has neither a beginning nor ending.

The Cat Outside His Door, # 4

And yet he sits, head raised, looking in.
Do you see? Do you know? Do you care?
Will you get up & walk down the hall?
I'm just around the corner, right here

only two blocks from where they laid
him to rest, just yards away from fields
Roethke walked through passing this way
once or twice. Can't you tell it's me

you want? Here, look around the corner,
out in the back, over here in the dark,
waiting for the sun to come up,
for one morning glory to open,

its petals uncurling one by one.
This song & dance is not nearly done.
In fact, it's not for you; it's something
I had to walk straight through.

So, it's nearly nonsense, I know, with little
rhyme, light rhythm, & a wall that's too tall.

The Cat Outside His Door, # 5

It is hard to tell just how long he sat there,
just sat, relaxed, alert, looking in, patiently
waiting for exactly what no one else seemed
to know, much less really care. So, there

he sat, while Roethke performed, carrying
on as if nothing else mattered, nothing else
was as significant as his reading, his uttering
his lines, singing his lyrics with more gusto

than ever before. Or so it all seemed to any
in the area during the taping and most viewers
later on when the film appeared. Ah, but can
we be certain what the connection between

poet and feline, what the subtle force drawing
them together then and lasting how long few
know, or even begin to understand. After all,
this cat is in the long tradition going back to

Egypt at least, and few comprehend the role
of felines back then, must less in Ted's day.

The Cat Outside His Door, # 6

> *"All learning is remembering and the lessons
> learned are but memories reclaimed."*
> —*Joe McNair*

There is much to be said for studying the
pharaohs, for in truth, when one searches
for wisdom, one could do less than take a
page or two from King Tut and others from

the Valley of the Kings and their era. Even
as a youngster I recall learning a minuscule
amount of Egyptian history, something about
the river Nile, about some ancient queens,

and then we also learned about hieroglyphics
and their purpose, their use, their meanings.
And shortly thereafter I began learning of
poets and poetry, in elegies and epigrams, as

I recall these many years later. Yes, after
acquiring a brief view of the beauty of Egypt,
I started reading the likes of Shelley and Keats,
Frost and Shakespeare, and, Roethke. Later, as

he, Roethke, was filmed reading in Puget Sound,
a cat sat outside his door just quietly looking in.

The Cat Outside His Door, # 7

Today it is hard to recall exactly just why that cat
sat outside that door while Roethke pranced inside
for the cameras, rattling off selection upon selection.
Amazing as it seemed then listening to his singing,

or nearly chanting, as it seemed, he spouted forth
love poem, family narrative, darkly tuned lyric,
and even Puget Sound and Michigan-grounded
life-like glimpses of tree, fern, rose, and bird. Oh,

he was very clear-throated, lumberjack nurtured, and
slightly mono-toned, so nattily attired, and mentally
focused, that he invoked the tradition of the medieval
court jester, the chanticleer spreading the word, or the

apprentice craftsman fashioning swords for a prince.
How clearly I recall his movements, his introductions
for each poem—being none of them over nor under-
stated or presented. A virtual performer was this

poet before his cat—that one waiting patiently outside
for its master enacting his singular chorus lines inside.

The Cat Outside His Door, # 8

for Carmen

Yes, it is true, the cat sat outside his door, sat
there all afternoon, perhaps all day, I can't be
too sure. And all the while Roethke carried on
as if he didn't notice, and probably that is so,

for he was known to not notice things when he
was so riveted on something that he failed to see
such as right in front of himself. Oh, I too do
know exactly what that is like, to just not quite

see, to not even begin to feel what you know
all too clearly when the muck is truly up to your
knee. When the parakeets chirp, chirping that is
as loud as rush hour horn blowing. Indeed, it

is just so easy to miss or misunderstand even
when trying to comprehend how it might feel
to be in one another's shoes; but, of course, that
isn't ever really possible, to feel as another does,

whether you or me. Ah, but we have each other,
yes, we do, and our love makes all the difference.

There Was a Cat Outside His Door

There Was a Cat Outside His Door, # 1

Now, I wonder if he still sits outside that door,
now that his master has left the premises?
What do you think, you who never ventured
close to the Sound, nor even heard his last song?

Is it possible, I muse, since Roethke, though deceased,
long ago, may be lingering—his spirit very present,
somehow still impinging upon the natural forces?
Could it be that his last dance is as long as a cat's

tail, tailored to fit into any pub or bar routine,
just before the night's last call? Here, I pause,
mulling over the full beauty of the night's rising moon
with it's bright white light outlining the lake's edge.

Sometimes a cat has more sense than man, other
times not seemingly half as smart as an inchworm,
but most of the time, patient or impatient, a cat
knows wherein the sun's rays spread its heat.

Ah, would that a man or woman could use such
cat-like intuitive knowing to understand others.

There Was a Cat Outside His Door, # 2

He, the cat, did just sit there waiting and waiting,
even as I sit here thinking, writing and feeling.
Somehow feeling that each day brings more and
more moments of hope, more golden opportunities

than yesterday and days gone by. Yes, I often
believe that when the sirens sang, perched as
they were upon those cliff rocks, not even Moses
could have dislodged them, caused them to quiet.

Now, looking out the sliding door, I see the new
yellow orchid, its stamen reaching toward the lake,
a mouth agape. I also notice the smaller orchid,
a pale cream shade, demure in appearance, shy

in its stationary position, off in the shadows, with
perhaps a penchant for attention. Isn't it odd
sometimes how one tends to overlook the clearly
recognizable, that is right in front of one's nose?

Roethke worked his wonders with words, with poems
until, finding the right voice, he stopped, wrote, stayed.

There Was a Cat Outside His Door, # 3

Yes, it is true, I did see the photos of him sitting there,
outside that door, never again opened by the poet;
unable to enter, unable to exit, unable to hear the voice
so distinct, and now though not quite quiet, no longer

the booming projection of the performer Roethke was.
I've heard it said that Albert Schweitzer moved through
the jungles until, discovering a treatment, in a place,
he stopped, stayed, working as long as needed.

Early this morning, looking out through the glass doors,
I wait for the Easter sunrise; I wait for my lover to appear.
Now, sitting here, I watch the mother duck bring her three
tiny ducklings—two a fuzzy brown, the other a chicken

yellow all over its hand-held size body—down to the
lake's edge to bathe, to feed, to explore. The tiny
birds stay close to the warmth of this feminine beast,
they draw close with their short legs working like crazy

when only six inches provides a gap between. Love we
grow into, like ducklings, learning to swim by doing.

There Was a Cat Outside His Door, # 4

Just as the cat sat so patiently outside his door,
now these several years ago, outside this glass door
I watch the duck take her three miniscule ducklings
down to the lake to feed, to peck and feed,

then back up under a bush to sleep, to rest, out of sight,
secure from any unwanted prey, out of the hawk's,
out of the vulture's view. This mother of winged
swimmers, not unlike the humans peopling Degas'

canvases--these many dancers captured in varying
hues of blue and green, she's poised to instruct, to teach,
from sunrise to dusk, as long as necessary until her
young charges can fend for themselves, sustain life

without aid in whatever weather Mother Nature
brings around. It was the spring and summer birds,
the muck and mire of Michigan woods, the quiet
of the forested Puget Sound area; it was the voice

of natural connection, the note of life in each flower,
wild or tame, Roethke recorded doing so exactly.

There Was a Cat Outside His Door, # 5

Even if he was still somehow sitting there outside his door,
I seriously doubt that even a Buddha would realize
that in order to be fully present in the moment, one—either
the cat or the poet—would have become spirit enough

that, although felines do have a sixth sense about them,
they often cause we humans to wonder if they have
a direct connection to the pharaohs in terms of possessing
a breadth and depth of learning especially of ritual and medicine,

and which could put we mortals to shame. Ah, when Roethke
was writing in tribute to Yeats and Stevens, his distinct
voice held such a musical quality that much of his verse
lends itself to singing and stage performance. Subjects like

the forested birds—jays, sparrows, hawks; the small
field mice; the lake pickerel and brook trout; the spinney pines,
aging oaks, and spreading maples; and the roots of wildflowers,
all gathering together in orchestral rehearsal, caught his fancy.

Perhaps the cat tuned in like a concertmaster and Prufrock's
ageless love song quest are somehow kindred spirits.

There Was a Cat Outside His Door, # 6

Perhaps when Roethke noticed the cat outside his door,
he realized that even this small creature was a kindred soul.
Perhaps when the cat outside his door sat watching
this poet performing his verses, his lines, his songs,

he couldn't but help tilt his head just a bit, listening
harder, listening closer, hearing just a might more
as the writer dotted his end stops, crossed his pitch and
raised his volume the better to be heard by such audience.

Perhaps, but not quite sure, I now recount my encounters
with this my poet, while revisiting a home town center,
with memory of the cemetery where they laid him out,
with the very roots, the branches, the flowers, the dirt

in which he reposes snug within that box, within that coffin
he was transported in from the Puget Sound area back to
his Michigan, back to this my native state also. Yet, there
is something not quite the same in this memory—in my

recall of the creeks, the small streams, and the bold nursery blooms,
and even in the verses so structured, even cats hear his voice.

There Was a Cat Outside His Door, # 7

How still he seemed to sit back then when Roethke read,
performing inside the house in front of the mantle, his head
tilted slightly as if listening more intently while the poet
stretched, reaching for just the right accent, the just right

volume level, using the just right gesture, the spontaneous
but just right swaying motions—the body moves of this
always anxious yet confident man, sometimes a bit too
concerned with the rhythms of others' work, too much

struck by the compelling critic's observations or audience
response. After all, just as the cat, whether looking in or out,
seems to weather any kind of attention, the poet seeks never
ending devotion, never ending recognition, continuing

acclaim, always needing, always wanting more than before.
Each new line, each depiction of any one of the earthen
elements, each description of birds, of small creatures,
fish in stream, brook or river, each novel twist of symbol

magnifying connections between man and nature, between
God, man and nature, still lingers in my reading of his poems.

There Was a Cat Outside His Door, # 8

Oh, I know now that when he used to sit outside the door,
he had an inquisitive look on his face, his eyes were wide
in an inquiring fashion, his whiskers in perfect alignment,
his grey tail wrapped neatly around his lower extremities,

although Roethke may not have been aware of this exactness,
of the precision with which the cat paused next to the screen
looking in. I don't believe there really was a Wicked Witch
of the West. Perhaps the eternal contest between the forces

of the environment—earth and wind—mesh so well that
there was no such spirit to cause the Woodman to throw
a bucket of water on? Perhaps, but who knows for certain,
for there is an untold story of Dorothy—the one having nothing

to do with Kansas or she returning in a hot air balloon.
Yes, my poet was familiar with nursery rhymes, with a ditty
or two, and could match symbol to image line after line. Then,
too, it just may be that Gretel was fashioning a wholly unique

tale or two just about the same time as she and Hansel took
their forest stroll. Ah, but does the cat still hear Roethke's voice?

There Was a Cat Outside His Door, # 9

Whenever I think about it, I very nearly see the cat sitting
still outside his door. And I usually then pause to ponder
on the wonder of it all—how a cat, long dead, appears
so vividly within my dreams, within my vision, within

my psyche for therein he seems to linger. When I was
a child I wandered through fields, alongside creeks, in
and out of woodlots, searching out minnows, water spiders,
chipmunks, cardinals, jays, and the stray occasional fox.

When I discovered Roethke's flowers, his meadow mouse,
the slow moving sloth, the strong pull of nature's lore,
I entered another world, one I was already quite a part of.
The tiny blue bells, the dapper black-eyed Susan, the delicate
Queen Anne's lace, and quaint Indian Pipes, all within my

view, within my woodlot and field walks, opened nature's
seam—providing an avenue into my connections, my role,
my responsibilities to our environment, to ourselves.
One of our cats once calling a former house home left in

time, moving into a neighbor's because too many other cats
took up residence in our abode. Not so Roethke's cat.

There Was a Cat Outside His Door, # 10

Years ago he worked at his craft, fashioning verses,
cutting out his childhood days, recognizing his father's
strength, learning while observing a quiet family cat,
and eventually capturing his affection for a young wife.

All this activity, all his attention, whether to plants,
to fowl, to fish, to tiny creatures underground, or even
to the love of his life—a delicate creature, a real beauty
culled from among his many admirers, his adoring public.

And then Roethke had this ability to recreate, to bring
to life, unlike no other writer I've known, the supple leaf,
the unexplored roots and often gnarled tree branches
aging in woodlots of the Sound, in forests of his Michigan.

Then, he worked; now, he is appreciated, respected for
what he accomplished, for the finely tuned edges of sound,
for the fascinating symbols drawn from nature—the rose,
the mouse, the trout. And there was that cat outside his door.

Ah, I am but beginning, starting, having been given such
an opportunity, to enjoy my love, young, lively as she is.

There Was a Cat Outside His Door, # 11

Years ago, I watched the poet's cat sit there. Now, I don't
know if he might still be lingering in the neighboring woods,
if his spirit has become somehow more intertwined with
the poet's own, and if the two are now more connected?

I never had the opportunity to walk through the ferns nor
pass the Buddha as Roethke did. Sheltered in a sweatshirt,
he absorbed the flavor of the plants, the delicate wildflowers,
the seasonal budding leaves and branches, each first nibbling

first poking through their skin, then gulping in fresh air
and scarce sunlight. He, the poet, took naturally
to the far west with its open skies, starlit nights,
smog free air, and lots populated with Douglas

firs – their bark a reddish brown and rough fluted, and the
Western hemlocks with their acorn size light brown cones.
Wandering, as he did, into woodlots and fields filled with
lady ferns and their delicate light green fronds, and

maidenhair ferns with black vertical stems, he found
places for some in lines, images, and in songs.

There Was a Cat Outside His Door, # 12

How back then it seemed so ironic that he wrote about Oakwood,
about watching and missing the passing horse drawn black hearses;
ironic that there he too would rest that day back in 63. I remember
spending part of a day trying to locate his grave site. I'm not sure

that I really actually wanted to. After all, what would I have
done then, what would I have said had I stood there alongside
his head stone? Instead, I moved on, not realizing I would
never be back, that I'd never return to his hometown, never

retrace his footsteps, never again pass by his family nursery,
nor retouch the trees in those woodlots, walk through those fields,
find quite the same edge when I touch the Michigan wildflowers,
watch the same small critters on the surface of streams, notice those

field mice scurry across open spaces, see the hawk dive for its
unsuspecting prey, hear the jay-jaying of nature's blues, observe
the cardinal pair—their colors at once bright and dull. Roethke
still prowls there, he gives meaning to the muck and mire of the

land, and his spirit resides there with or without the cat or the
cat's spirit at least. So, now, what am I left to do?

There Was a Cat Outside His Door, # 13

I've read that the hummingbird beats its wings 60-80 times
a second when in flight. I wonder how fast its small heart
pumps when it is resting? Of all the mysteries of nature,
of all the magical qualities uncovered, yea, discovered by

all the scientists studying known creatures, or poets' verses
extolling their virtues, I never quite just wondered which
is the most awesome, which more remarkable, which truly
the most fantastic one of all. Perhaps it's the smallest web

spider spinning its lines in order to corner its unsuspecting
prey? Maybe it's the slow moving snail inching across a
morning sidewalk? Could that be Roethke's field mouse
darting across the open field, unprotected and avoiding

all its natural predators? How long does the average small
ant survive in its anthill? Can one even begin to actually
measure the kind of quality of sound attributed to blue jays
on the wire? Isn't it just possible that without the aid of all

our devices, without use of all our technology, without our
often coveted skills, the poet's cat does somehow still live?

There's No Cat Outside My Door

There's No Cat Outside My Door, #1

There is something to be said for having one's cat
waiting each morning outside the door, for knowing
that the animal is as steady, as sure, as faithful as
the poet's pen was in turning small critters into images,

night-calling birds into symbols, ferns into gardens,
wild flowers into poetic lines, bent and twisted trees
into stanzas, and then into lyrical poems resounding
with cries of the dense forested Sound area outside

his home. Yes, Roethke was as faithful to his art,
to his work and craft as that cat to his then master.
How seldom is the bond ever broken, almost never
severed while both still live. But, what happens after

when one dies, when one is removed from the physical
presence, from the habitat wherein the other remains?
Can the spirit, the so abstract connection between man
and beast, between craftsman and artful creature survive?

I, too, in an oft-chance sort of manner, have been removed
from creature bonds by distance, so do I maintain a link?

There's No Cat Outside My Door, #2

I don't remember looking recently, but the last time I did there was
no cat outside my door. There was however, just last night, a small
ugly-looking statue, apparently left there by some passerby, perhaps
someone unable to carry their load any further, and so being near

my doorstep, left this object for me to discover as I did upon my
arrival from visiting friends. I remember the delight I had the day
I first recognized a Queen Anne's lace while walking across the field
on my way to school; it was like learning how to take a perfect photo.

Now I know there is nothing quite like my young discoveries, my
   being
able to spot, then know one wildflower from another and name
   them.
Surely Roethke must have experienced such things as he grew up in
nearly the same Michigan fields and woodlots, not far from where I

later came to live. He listened to the jay-jaying, watched the scurrying
of mice across open spaces darting from the eye of the hawk, the
   vulture.
And then, too, he climbed atop nursery greenhouses, slid down dirty
snow banked hillsides, breathed in the spring fresh air of April and
   May.

Yesterday when you turned over and lay there looking at me with
your smile, you took me back and then forward into dream visions.

There's No Cat Outside My Door, #3

Okay, I admit that since the cat has been missing for
two weeks, there's little chance he will return. After
all, it isn't like the times when he went next door and
would curl up at the foot of the neighbor's baby crib

providing just the right kind of security for the infant,
just the right kind of oversight during its sleep, and
just the natural amount of love, if it is that, between
creature and child, expressed in the only way this cat

could—by insuring that no other thing disturbed this
newborn, at least during his reign at bedside. Of course,
Roethke did write of the helpless and hapless creature
separated from its mother, not abandoned, and crossing

a field alone, nearly unable to discern a safe space from
natural predators having not yet learned either what to
expect nor when to run and hide. Even the sloth hanging
upside down, suspended in sleep, has a means, instinct,

of gathering in rather than becoming mere bait, mere
subject for stronger, more fit, bigger to take it down.

There's No Cat Outside My Door, #4

I've often wondered when he would endure a bout
of manic depression, which then no doctor knew how
to treat, no shrink had a remedy handy to at least aid
in providing him with a means of lessening what he

had to struggle through, what he had to find his own
way out with only limited assistance, with just enough
security to keep him safe, to provide him sustenance
as he sought to write his way back to full recognition,

back to the creative state he so craved, the balance
he so avidly sought. Roethke needed every bit of the
energy he witnessed in both his father's dirt-encrusted
hands, and his uncle's concern with natural growth,

a growth that was very nearly a family trait, not unlike
a heirloom some clans treasure generation to generation.
There were cats around the nursery, but one cat sat near
outside his door in the Sound area, a quiet observer.

Again this morning there is no cat outside my door;
I don't believe the neighbors let theirs out very often.

There's No Cat Outside My Door, #5

There's one rose in the vase; its deep pink shade brings
out the detail in delicate petals. When Roethke wrote
of the rose, a rose in the sea wind of the Puget Sound
area, he described its strength, its vitality, its energy.

But the poet also recalled his father and childhood
greenhouses and the multiple rows of roses and the
cement benches filling the ends of long sets of pots.
Both the rose struggling, surviving near rocks, near

the sea in the winds, and the man-nurtured potted
roses gathering measured waters in and jutting high
their three to four foot stems protruding into spaces
protected from cruel Michigan winters, shaded in hot

summer days, cultivated night and day, managed with
the family tough love displayed throughout growing
years, influencing the young poet unto his death. His
flowers depicted with a grasp, an understanding few

ever gain. Even if there was a cat outside my door I
doubt its staying power could surpass a rose in the night.

There's No Cat Outside My Door, #6

The geranium didn't wilt until it was tossed onto
the slag heap, the crow didn't alight until it neared
the power lines, the slug didn't move very far in
the afternoon heat, and the cat didn't wake for an hour.

Whenever Roethke wrote his exacting lyrics, whether
love songs or narratives cataloging nature's creatures,
he used roses, unnamed things, small field mice,
among varied objects as symbolic of the growing

strength of focused tender care and devotion. Family
and friends, poets and their audiences, cats and their
owners, birds and their prey, professors and their
students, editors and their writers—all have one

thing in common, and that's giving and taking, the
longing and the making of love, the love in learning.
When he drafted a poem touching the roots of a plant,
edging the strength of a rose growing, or the stem of a

fern—those filling his space, his environment, either
in Michigan or in the Sound—he carefully etched life.

There's No Cat Outside My Door, #7

When a friend posed the question—what's the great imperative of my life?—this is too significant a matter to ignore. Is it important when I write to always have an audience, to obtain vital feedback, genuine critical

responses? Or is it sufficient to only be able to read my work with such understanding that in doing so, as Roethke claimed, I am coming as close as it is possible to recreating the essence of the poem?

I used to wonder why he left that cat outside his door and if the reason might have been that somehow his Buddha stood between them or if it was just that this single cat was merely a player off-stage, not a sage

with any message to deliver. How still shrouded is some of the mystery, the wonder, the analysis of the levels of meaning in some of his final poems, some of his best work yet left open for deeper examination.

Again today, when I open my door I find no cat and not even a trace that one came by in the night. Why?

There's No Cat Outside My Door, #8

When I was young I admired those who could figure
skate; now as I age I find I still appreciate those
who can. Today a friend buried her pet dog,
yesterday another friend's father passed away at 92,

and the day before yet another friend's dad died after
a long, sad struggle with cancer. Sometimes I just sit
here waiting for the phone to ring wishing you'd call
and talk with me, wanting but to hear your voice

in my ears, looking so forward to doing so that oft
times I nearly try to will it so—that the telephone
will indeed ring, ring only until I pick it quickly up.
I'm never too sure when I sit at the computer if what

is in my thoughts, what is working around in brain
patterns will or won't find its way into something
less than a puzzle, something quite different from
when a mother cat suckles its newborn kitten giving

the love only the mother can. Yes, if I can learn but
half of what Roethke shows in poems, I will live.

There's No Cat Outside My Door, #9

First I moved the shelves over along the side wall,
then I found a place for the small wine rack, the
pedestal with the classic head upon it, and finally
the Native American made drum. Eventually, I

decided it was essential to shift the knick-knack
cabinet being careful not to disturb your angels,
your unicorns or your various associated other
collectables. I wonder if the neighbor's cat is

outside or just sitting in a window looking out?
I supposed, unlike Roethke's cat which sat some-
what patiently looking in the screen door while
the poet performed his ballads and love songs,

that such focused creatures, unlike we humans,
rarely lose their compunction to complete a task
whatever it may be. I opened the door a crack
late last night and just now again this morning,

but there was no cat, and there isn't any cat outside
my door then or now. So a cat sits in this poem.

There's No Cat Outside My Door, #10

I remember the dream very well. In it there was no
door. There was a long, long hallway stretching
down deeper and deeper into what seemed to be a
cave, and the lower and further I went the damper

and darker it got until I could very nearly taste the
moisture in the air. But every now and then I did
a reality check, for I knew that I was not caught up
in a Edgar Allan Poe maelstrom from the way the

walls continued to rise straight up from the edges
of the floor. Of course, like Roethke's cat was
once outside looking in, Poe had a cat appearing
within one of his gloom and doom stories, and this

weird cat just seemed to slip in and out of my dream
now and again. Yes, somehow I caught occasional
glimpses of this feline as I slipped deeper and deeper
into my sleep. Then, sometime before daylight, when

I realized I was dreaming, I got up, moved down a
real hall, opened the outside door, and saw no cat.

There's No Cat Outside My Door, #11

Unlike the girl in the story, the little boy didn't like
to eat green eggs and ham; in fact, not many people
like to eat things such as that. But, late in the evening
when I have a craving for something to munch on, I

sometimes search for the silly things—chicken wings
and wine, sausage and peanut butter on crackers, small
pieces of sweet orange candies with coke. I suppose
these yearnings, unnatural or not, stave off boredom.

This morning, during my walk, I mildly rebuked one
bold black cat intent on chasing another from his top
porch step perch—his previous evening's resting place—
and happily he abandoned his attack, retreating slowly

into the bush-darkened house side. I barely paused,
not wishing to loose my stride, while only also thinking
whether Roethke's cat had its moments when the poet
wasn't around. Yes, sometimes, creatures enter another's

terrain without invitation, plowing ahead, blithely
venturing wherein often it has no business, none at all.

There's No Cat Outside My Door, #12

All of a sudden, it was just there at the lake's edge,
all three plus feet tall of it – the big grey/blue heron
in the morning's sunlight, its wings spread triangle
like, open to air and sun dry, its body turning with the

changing directional movement of this early sun.
Never having seen such a fowl creature so fully
extended, nor so close, I gasp at the natural beauty
of this one of God's creatures, such a wonder, such

a perfect work of art, sculpted by the master of all
artists. I remember how carefully and completely
Roethke use to craft his images, his lines, his poetic
portraits of hapless creatures – the small, the tiny,

the nearly forsaken vermin littler than even his cat.
The poet's 'thing' – the unnamed bird so distant as to
be an unspecified species (in his poem) – diving on its
unsuspecting prey, striking at the very last minute with

as much accuracy and as swiftly as my daughter's cat
or even as the poet's in its heyday out near the Sound.

There's No Cat Outside My Door, #13

Some days pass by so quickly I hardly know they're gone;
during other times, especially if I am aware of a clock
or a watch, the hours, even the very minutes during which
I may be searching for something interesting to read or

looking for an exciting movie to view, such a passage
moves ever so slow. Perhaps one of those days was when
I saw both John Wayne in his *Cowboy* film and Gene
Hackman in the *French Connection* film. Actually, both

are quality works, but neither can quite be compared with
a rereading of Roethke's *The Far Field* collection. An
hour attempting to recreate the flavor of his contemplations
of the self in his very powerful, complex North American

Sequence poems is more rewarding. When the poet has
reached this stretch of work, this point in his creative life,
he is seeking to illuminate his "I" and such is not easy.
Yet to the degree he ever does so, he anguishes as he

unravels his tangled, disturbed nature until this becomes
as clear as the cries of the cat no longer outside my door.

Did You See That Cat?

Did You See That Cat? #1

It has been a difficult day from the time
I got up this morning until I sat down to
record this set of experiences. First, the
clouds opened up early and let loose

some rain, just enough to chase the cat
back inside the neighbor's porch. Then,
for some reason, I forgot to take your
lunch when I went out the door. So, by

now I not only missed my early walk,
but I had to turn around and backtrack
to pick up the food. I don't know what
Roethke's cat did when it suddenly rained,

but I suspect he didn't just sit by the door
and wait to be let in. And, after all, both
cat and poet had other things to be about.
Me too, so, in spite of feeling lonely in

midday, I daydream of being happy,
then sit down and write this poem.

Did You See That Cat? #2

This morning watching the colors of the sun
catch the growing daylight clouds was like
observing the sand paintings out in the deserts
of New Mexico or the various canyons as the

late summer sunrise catches edges of desert
cliffs or the walls of national park deep river
cut streams drawing out vibrant shades of light
green, various hues of baby blues, faint pinks,

soft yellows, and other assorted cosmic views
so like masters' oil paintings or subtle watercolors.
Yes, it is but an amazing assortment of brilliant
yet subdued riches of light catching and high-

lighting the varied scenes. Now, I remember a
wild cat, a Canadian lynx, passing through our
campground during the night, so I missed seeing,
only hearing it. The closest to wild cats might be

the foxes I see here in South Florida. Of course
they aren't cats, at least not like Roethke's own.

Did You See That Cat? #3

The afternoon passed quickly, conversation
turning slowly into foreplay, then broaches
of sentiment becoming a kiss and a peck,
whether on cheek or neck, on forehead or ear.

Where earlier we spoke of your daily banking
woes in a workaday world, the anxious ones
you sought to satisfy with consummate service
or the staff sometimes prone to forget or stop

just short of completing a task however small
it might seem. But, back to our communion,
to our disposition of frolic before dinner, in
search of other expressions, other renderings

of feelings, offerings of emotions—gentle
and fulfilling, august and giving, erstwhile
and projecting. Not unlike kittens playing,
washing and pawing, lapping and chewing,

we approach each other with eyes wide open,
Roethke-like, expressing, wanting and sharing.

Did You See That Cat? #4

When is it that the mother cat cuts loose its kitten,
knowing it will be okay, somehow surviving? Is it
like Roethke writing of a feline, knowing when to
end lines? Or is it more like the mouse seeking safe

passage across the meadow not being too sure when
or if its predator will show or just where or when it
does? Well, even the poet, rendering this narrative
can't be too sure, observing the tale, just how this

story will conclude or exactly what the outcome will
be, whether the hapless victim or relentless prey shall
preserve—which one will survive. Ah, but, we humans
have a different perspective, another more objective

view of more directly the nature of the outcome than
the tiny unsuspecting creature seeking only a peaceful
passage in its unmerciful kingdom. Yes, the poet did
write of these things—of the inanimate flowers and

objects, of the innocent objectives of circling vultures,
of the kitten abandoned by its mother, dead in morning.

Did You See That Cat? #5

It isn't quite a full moon yet; tomorrow or Tuesday,
I think. But the light on the lake is bright tonight,
the edges touching the surface almost as if from
a flashlight, highlighting the small, quiet ripples.

And talking with you earlier, just before you were
going to return to sleep, hearing the soft, lulling
sound of your voice, feeling the love in your voice,
making the connection, even if only on the phone.

Yes, today is a good day; the storm clouds didn't
bring in the rain. Perhaps it will during the night;
the nearly silent noise of raindrops while sleeping
is a soothing tool, one I sometimes need to heal.

The days are growing shorter, daylight coming
later; dusk appearing earlier, nearly before dinner
is over. Roethke, too, writes of love and waters;
and of small creatures, especially mice, snakes.

But you, my dear, have a way of purring not unlike
a cat, one of mine, not his; such as love brings on.

Did You See That Cat? #6

Not knowing if these days of waiting, this time
in between, when waiting, always with anticipation,
is harder to do, something I am rather anxious about
while knowing you are out there and not yet here,

not yet herein with me. I find passing the interim
taxes my brain waves, and I am not quite sure if
my writing is getting easier or more difficult than
I have ever known before. Yes, watching the ducks

moving around the edge of the lake is intriguing;
they are, after all, teaching their young ducklings
to fend for themselves, showing them safe methods
of approaching other extended families without, quite

like an eagle on its nest surveying the surrounding
woods and meadows, alert to small creatures—the
hapless and solitary ones scurrying across the forest
floor or the open fields. I wonder just how good a

hunter Roethke's cat was--if he, like the poet, stayed
with his object until he was able to capture it whole?

Sitting With Theodore Roethke

Sitting With Theodore Roethke, #1

Rereading memorable lines about
his meadow mouse, his geranium, his song-bearing birds,
I walk out into the yard, stand under
the bottlebrush tree and listen hard for Roethke's wind.

Mother and her mother before her
held and played this violin,
but one day I just set it down carefully
and haven't picked it back up since.

Listening to Brahms, nearing the edge of sleep,
I long to nod off and do not stir before
dawn's light, to rest, to restore energy, to dream
until daylight slips in between the blind's slats.

When I was younger I fancied being a mountaintop lookout,
watchful for nature's summer lightning strike fires,
mindful that solitude is a pleasant thing, solstice being
something that might yield a natural understanding, a satori.

Sitting With Theodore Roethke, #2

Standing transfixed by the twisting, turning, twirling
carousel of dancing and prancing horses,
unable to lift even one foot, one leg, I yearn for those river
evenings when dangling earthworms from Grandpa's bamboo poles.

Meandering down halls lined with assorted watercolors,
chalked wildflower-filled fields, and pencil-etched portraits,
I step off on an angle toward glassed exit doors
humming notes of a childhood nursery ditty.

Ah, moonlight coming in the window is filtered by leaves,
softened by light breezes whispering around the house from the east,
and spreading out over the far wall providing a faint illumination.
Perhaps, as elders believe, the life of a tree is the life of me.

When you speak of hiking up the mountain slope to the lodge,
I can't help but wonder about the wildflowers, the wild berries;
darting, chirping birds, and small four-pawed creatures underfoot
all surviving in harmony, somehow, with the poet, with us.

Again and again, the more I read, the greater my understanding,
as I stretch for Roethke's edges, I reach for the very spirit of my self.
I am beginning to sense the impact in my veins, in my being.
Yet, no doubt, Roethke's search remains ragged in his death.

Sitting With Theodore Roethke, #3

Tonight sleep seems just a notch away, out of reach,
probably because I am working, and I'm not quite
used to this 4 o'clock hour. Other days, other nights,
whichever, as tired as I might then seem and be,
it often feels difficult, if not impossible, to doze off,
for sleep does not come easy to a cluttered mind.

What is it about a dream that I slip into and out of
between sleep and waking? And how come I can't
as easily reenter it when it's disrupted by some slight
sound or by a sudden involuntary jolting movement.
Perhaps Freud would have a quick or complex answer,
perhaps not. Some answers are not easy to come by,
and perhaps it's unnecessary to know everything anyway.

As I recall Roethke often had to struggle with an abyss,
a sense of slipping into or being within the unknown.
He frequently wrote his way out of such, recovering
with lines of allegorical references, all to further ID
his own persona, pinning down that which often
remains allusive, that which we don't know and
sometimes never discover with much certainty.
I wonder, is one's insight richer in an afterlife?

Theodore Roethke in Michigan

Theodore Roethke in Michigan, #1

for Katie, in Michigan

Shortly after sunrise in the middle of June
I walk into the field heading toward the small creek.
Slowly moving through the clumps of weeds,
I notice the delicate beauty of Queen-Anne's Lace,
the occasional young daisies, their dainty petals
small, pointed and opening in the early sunlight.

When Roethke walked in the fields outside his hometown,
he reached deep into the muck of many summer rains,
stretching to capture the essence, the very art
of each plant along his way. This morning as
I make my path through this meadow-like area,
I feel the very pulse of his Michigan world, now
also my own, in the strands of grasses underfoot,
in the color of bluebells and smell of creek side moss.

Whatever it is, whatever it takes to fashion,
to gather as possession, however momentarily,
I find, take, briefly borrowing, and then seek to return
whether in spoken word or in poetic image and line.
To absorb and remit, to garner, comprehend and
give back out remains a wonder, oft-times nearly a puzzle,
for my sighting is minuscule in contrast to the masters
whether on canvas, in photographs or in verse.
For a tiny moment, I seek to breathe in and out fresh air.

Theodore Roethke in Michigan, #2

Some wild daisies dot the meadow clearing;
a morning glory, alongside the little traveled trail,
opens in the growing eastern sunrise;
and wood geraniums, their bright violet five-part
petals are caught in the early day's light.

I follow this mountain forest path
rising up from the fields below from the
canoe landing next to the river down there.
As I move I can't help thinking of John Muir
traversing his California foothills or Henry David
Thoreau moving about in his Maine woods.

Of course, now, I also recall how Roethke tramped
through fields and woodlots of his Michigan just as
I do whenever I return to the same countryside.
And I wander alongside the small streams meandering
through groupings of wildflowers populated with
insects and other tiny creatures—all going about their
business, all unhampered by human interruption.

Theodore Roethke in Michigan, #3

for Duane Locke

This morning as I take the trash to the dumpster
I can't help but notice that directly in front of me
a line of ants moves across the walkway as if
they're squeezing space. I wonder what it takes
to move in such a concerted effort that no single
creature is disconnected from the rest. Their
activity at times so close it seems that were one
to stop, they'd be unable to adjust their movement
as minnows do in their watery schools swerving

first one way then another and back again while
avoiding objects protruding into their wet fishing
grounds. But, as I observe, I see a small group of
four or five ants take a bit of a side jaunt from the
line for only what seems a moment. It appears as
if they are either looking for something or perhaps
only avoiding objects in their path too minuscule
for me to view clearly. Funny how we humans

have habits not unlike some of our small creatures,
these ants or the snails more independent in their
travels sometimes crossing sidewalks too, or the not
quite so small worms trailing across cement leaving
glistening marks behind. We two-legged, upright
figures, having evolved from uncouth, hair-pulling
cave dwellers into princely clothed, socially-elite
CEOs or neighbor backyard grilling sports grunts,
or paid and unpaid willing writer, performer. Such
was Roethke, my poet, and I, the now aging novice.

Theodore Roethke in Michigan, #4

The many areas in which Roethke wandered as
a youth, once open fields and friendly porched
homes, now barely noticeable as urban filled spaces
no longer available for a Saturday afternoon young
man's foray in search of nature's wonders, offer
little to either sustain a curiosity or raise time's
questions or even cause one to pause long enough
to assay disconcerted thought less barely stir juices
in the matter of the poet's thirst for fodder providing
notes--in line after line, image upon image, or argument-
tethered ponderings yielding either narrative or lyric.

But, alas, in Michigan with this poet, perhaps we both
now would need to travel outside such unfamiliar
places in search of a meadow or meandering stream
or scarce woodlot attracting yet more than first catches
the eye—the mouse scurrying under decaying leaves,
the water bug's widening circles, or the squirrels
gathering nuts and then perched upon tree fallen logs.

It seems like it may be time for both of us to rest here,
tardy as we might be to a mother's dinner-time calling.
Too long we may have stopped here, revisiting decades,
seeking love and like, wanting but to hear and answer
the sounds echoing in these woods, turning in thought.
When will I find the answers, when will I know, as so
often Roethke seemed to wonder, if the abyss is too close.

Sometimes Theodore Roethke Just Slips into a Poem Meant for Another

Sometimes Theodore Roethke Just Slips into a Poem Meant for Another

for Carmen

I cherish such early summer mornings like this; the sun is barely coming up over the horizon and it is struggling to ease through some what may become storm clouds by afternoon. It is warm but not yet sweat hot, and though there is no hint of a breeze, the quiet of this hour is relaxing, even capturing the peace of nature's presence, especially of the many early birds not quite yet joined in their new day's first chorus. Nearly every time I am fortunate to take a walk out nearby and enjoy nature's bountiful offerings, you enter my thoughts. Not that you aren't somehow ever present in my mind. I am amazed each time you disrupt what I may be focused on; it is like walking through an open field and trying to notice each and every wild flower, each blade of each kind of many different grasses and then not forgetting even only one. Actually, it also very like, somehow, my efforts to write a poem as I attempt to quickly note my ideas in images, seeking to connect strains of lines and words without losing or messing up the natural flow. Yes, not unlike how Roethke must have worked through his notebooks distilling such varied impressions of his too natural surroundings either from woodlots outside his Michigan home site or in the Puget Sound areas out around his adopted Northwest residence. Somehow, as light slips into this morning's walk, you too appear within my enjoyment of nature's offerings—such comfort I find in each activity, such feelings herein to awaken me.

It Sounds Like Your Woodpecker Has Moved Into My Tree

Pardon me, it sounds like your woodpecker has moved over here into my tree.
Now, I hear him more clearly; the wood is supple, his pecking act intent.
This knocking above my head brings me up and out to feel the sun warming cool air,
to walk on lush rain-greened grasses, to sense a presence in this space.
Yes, your bird, my bird, it does not matter, for before the rain is felt, the tree is tall,
and after the gentle shower, I see it still with dark laden branches jutting out.
Again, I say, pardon me, it sounds like your woodpecker has moved over here
into my tree, and I, the lucky one, feel it in my chest, feel it in my fingers,
and so share too your song. And this bird's song, transmitted by tapping,
is stronger now than before, so my head and my body tell me.
When Roethke returned to his Michigan fields, walking on moss,
passing near wild roses, delicate summer flowers, did he too break into song,
or did he move over to the other side of a meadow seeking shade of the trees?

The Hillside Was Covered

What I remember most is that
the hillside was covered with dandelions
their sun yellow in stark contrast
to the deep, dark green stains of fresh
early summer grasses in which the
wild flowers were scattered
nearly as far as my eyes might see.

I walked slowly around the side
of this park hill and then up over the top
from which I could see the river's
bridge span just a short distance away.
I remember thinking that if I take the time
to cross over the waters
I will be headed homeward,
and on the way pass near to my mentor's
former home and not far from
the florist shop his family once supplied.

Though I never quite understood it then,
just being somewhere near the fields
he tramped as a youngster or when
home from college on holiday was something,
something I came later to sense in a lasting
impressionable manner. I used to wonder
if there were surviving bunches of wild roses
or perhaps even geraniums yet growing
in the space out behind his home.

And when I chanced upon a creek-like stream
wending it its way through the meadows
leading over to the woods running out
from the still open areas where greenhouses
used to stand I imagined Theodore there

either following the creek in search
of small critters, or listening for the jays
and cardinals, and noticing the hawks circling
along the edge of the forested section.

Oh, to have been along in early mornings
when Roethke might amble over the
creek banks, stopping to feel the smooth
and round leaves of wild ferns and
blow off the canopies of Queen Anne's lace,
I might then have started my botany
education much earlier in my youth.
How am I even now, as I wander
in and near his one time neighborhood
with these fields, streams and woodlots
and its now similar natural reminders
of my poet's having grown up here, to sense
even close to what he experienced then,
while I take in these unique natural wonders
of Michigan's fresh early and moist springs
and delightful flush green gently warming summers.
These days the hillside is covered, and the fields
are again populated with multiple rainbow colors.

Cats And Mothers Grow Somewhat Alike

'Oh, to be a mother, a gift like no other...'

for Carmen

When you were younger you became a mother, a mother eager
and loving, lovingly attached to your two sons, not unlike the
mother cat to her litter of kittens newly delivered in the closet
corner. The cat suckling its new born, you feeding your sons

each in turn, each provided the sustenance vital for growth,
vital for each one's development as each sought to greet, then
grasp the meaning of their surroundings, learning, and gathering
in knowledge—assorted information so necessary in daily life.

The mothering cat slowly, surely brings its litter out from its
lair, coaxing, then herding them—each one carefully so as not
to loose sight of any—until they become familiar with their
environment, preparing them either for eventually entering

the natural world outside the house, or to learn the inside outs
of the household domain pending its master's desires. Your
sons grow like stable trees sturdy, strengthened first by instinct,
yours, then theirs, and family coached information, then formal

schooling. Eventually both, sons and kittens, must break their
maternal bond, must find their own paths as did Roethke's cat.
It too eventually left its doorstep spot, its observation post,
whether to enter the opened screen or to snuggle under a step.

Sometimes, During The Rain

if one listens carefully at night it is possible
to hear the individual sound of each drop
as it falls ever so gently upon the grass
or the dirt off the edge of the porch. Perhaps
this is an activity more regular during a
summer's evening, although it is also very
possible during an afternoon's light shower
if the rain is not a heavy one and the drops
are not very big. Probably we are really
meant to share our earthly space with our
natural surroundings in such easy fashion.

Like when we were younger, in our
early growing years. Except, if we look
about carefully, listen with our eyes and
heart, make just a little effort to realize
how fortunate we truly are to share this
world with such as the delicate morning
glory opening in the growing sunlight
its blossom widening as the light focuses
clearly. And then too, in the time before
noon, when the sun moves high overhead,
and I'm walking through the field, more
meadow-like than not, and I come across
a Queen Anne's lace almost dainty in its
appearance or a sunflower, not a huge
one but a smaller more exact stem in its
standing, moving in the relaxing breeze.

The breeze caressing my cheek as I
gaze, intently upon these real wonders
of our environment. How is it that we
are permitted to connect with such as
these natural works of art that put the

likes of Monet, Cezanne and Degas in
awe, then impressing them to the degree
they sought to turn canvas into copies,
original as they are, seeking, connecting,
drawing us into their inspired worlds.
Yet, there is nothing to compare with
the first-hand encounter stopping in
the midst of a walk crossing through
an open meadow in a mid-summer's day
whether in the open rural countryside
or up on a plateau in the lower slopes
of Appalachian mountains while hiking
higher and higher seeking cloud mist.

Just how is it that I, the frail creature
I continue to be, am so embodied as to
experience such phenomena first-hand.
Maybe Frost had such an awareness
when he hesitated for a single moment
before taking the path meant for him.
Or Roethke taking note with so many
years of his father's song echoing in
his ears for nearly all of his too short
lifespan and spewing forth in his own
continuing volume of honored songs.
How am I to know all this, how too
can I bring more attention to others
sharing as I pass through my days.

Three Days Before Theodore Roethke Died

I just happened to be walking on a street
near the Roethke florist shop in Saginaw,
Michigan...near the greenhouse, the place
he learned so well the turns and twists
nature takes. The place in which he lived

and as a child danced round 'n round more
than once. A place with its muck, its
fossils, and even geraniums. The place
to which he returned again and again.
Yes, that's where I was walking, not in his

shoes—they were too large; he was a bear
of a man, lumbering in size, looming
head and shoulders over others. But I was
moving over cracked concrete, headed out
by the cemetery in which he was left later.

I lived nearby, and having discovered a few
of his poems a couple years before, I enjoyed
walking through the streets and fields he used.
I guess I thought I could feel something
of what he experienced in my being there.

Returning home the afternoon before he
died, I sat in a wingback chair before
a window looking out toward the river
not too far from where he must have stood,
and reading carefully, I joined his sloth,

serpent, kitty-cat bird, and lizard—all
his creatures, big and small, and then, by
chance, some roses, ferns, the roots and all
things beautiful, awakening in the soil.
Then, the next day I heard Roethke died.

Epilogue:

Somewhere, Somehow, Theodore, I Know

Somewhere, Somehow, Theodore, I Know

Remembering Theodore Roethke

You left me behind not giving me the opportunity
to speak with you, to thank you for the sheer pleasure
of visiting your life via your poetry. For the few
years I grew to know your work living in the area
you frequented as a youngster, wandering some of
the fields near your home, become the matter in your
writing, entering the namesake flower shop nearly
all that remains of your family fifedom along with
the family homestead now a preserved museum.

Other than the cemetery they laid you to rest in,
which I once wandered aimlessly about in search
of the soil spot above your six foot, six feet down
bear-like frame. I wanted to ask you questions,
to learn if my use of your work in classrooms was
to your liking, if I might just listen once to you
reading your own poems rather than my trying so
to imitate your voice from the shielded recording
in my possession all these years. I remember from
accounts by those privileged to sit in your university
rooms first-hand absorbing your approach to poetics,
to showing how one might feel the creative juices,
using the natural elements—the slug, the sloth,
the mouse, the jay, the earth and the waters—
fashioning image and idea, blending fire, wind
and water. And tempering, tampering, molding

with spirited feelings so much in a never-ending
quest praising our environment while in search
of oneself, seeking, ever searching for that illusive
answer trying to uncover *which I is I* amid those
moments you spent, we spend, uncovering much
that might stay lost, understandings of oft times

undiscovered knowledge as one writes the
unauthorized and unwritten autobiography.

Theodore, if I might so address, there are times
I feel my instinctive knack, an intuitive knowing
is close at hand, within my grasp only to sit
on a ledge of the open window through which
the bird's call and cry enters and semi-translates
your ideas, your powerful yet delicate word
and thought strongly enough for my recognition.

I cannot lament, for that is selfish, I can recall
my own pleasures in rereading, rediscovering
the intensity, the depth, the delightful depiction
of this graceful, yet unforgiving world in which
we inhabit woodlots and fields, the edges of lakes
and streams, feel the force of wind and the heat
of fire which you have so exactingly presented.
And I thank you now for how much more I know
from having buried myself in your life's work.

About The Author

Fred Wolven is a native of Theodore Roethke's home state, Michigan. The author discovered Roethke's poems in literary periodicals in 1957. Caught by Roethke's use of nature and his struggle to understand himself in his poems, Wolven began a lifetime study of his work. Living for a time in Saginaw, Roethke's hometown, near where he grew up, his family florist shop and greenhouses, and the fields he roamed as a youngster, Wolven took in Roethke's Midwestern roots and his fascination with nature. Wolven also realized Roethke's deep impact on contemporary poets and in his own writing as Wolven's poetry reflects a deep appreciation of nature and efforts to grasp more fully fundamentals of his own self in searching for the meaning of self.

In an extended teaching career, the author used Roethke's work and ideas. Thus, Wolven's writing evidences Roethke's influence in his use of nature and a probing for a clearer ID of himself. And nearly five decades later such remains a strong influence in Wolven's writing.